FIRST WISH

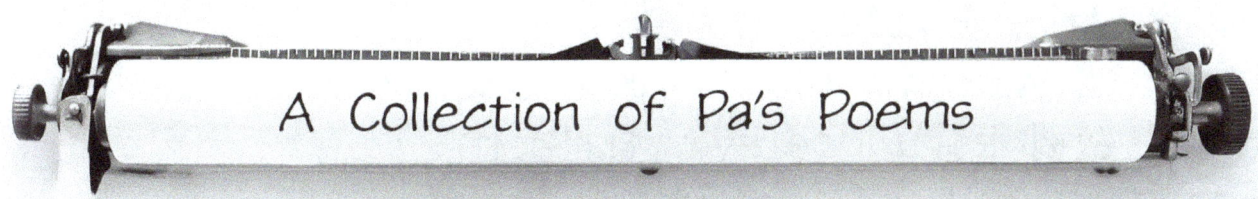

A Collection of Pa's Poems

Written by: Bud Endries

First Wish: A Collection of Pa's Poetry
Copyright 2024 Bud Endries
All rights reserved.
No part of this publication may be reproduced,
distributed, or transmitted in any form
or by any means, including photocopying,
recording, or other electronic or mechanical methods,
without prior permission of the publisher.
For permissions, contact:
endriesbudpoetry@gmail.com
Written by: Bud Endries
ISBN: 979-8-89316-524-1 - Paperback
ISBN: 979-8-89694-505-5 - Hardcover
ISBN: 979-8-89316-523-4 - eBook
First edition 2024
Visit: www.permacultureprincess.com/book
Email: endriesbudpoetry@gmail.com
Facebook Author Page: Bud Endries

Table of Contents

Copyright 1
Table of Contents 2
Dedication 3
A Note From The Author 4
Inspiration 5
Foreword 6
First Wish 7
Katydid 9
The "I Don't Know" Animal 11
Randy Roach 13
Sequoia 15
Spider Lived 17
That's a Croc 19
My Horse Plastic 21
Bird With A Flat Beak 23
Doctor Bill 25
Stingy Sue 27
Willows Flute 29
Ticklish Toes 31
Platypus 33
Some Just Don't Listen 35
The Web 37
We're All Nuts 39
Singing Worm 41
Ringing Will 43
The Protein Filled Apple 45
Apple Pie 47
Sue 49
Meow 51
What Do you Like 53
Sharing 55
Orange Breasted Robin 57
Dedicated Illustrator Page 59
Open Pages 61

"Dedicated to my wife, Judy, my children, Shane & Andrea, and all of my grandchildren, Silas, Sawyer, Shelby, Samarah, Stella, Montana, Solomon & Bridger."

A NOTE FROM THE AUTHOR

My prayer is that every child will grow up
feeling safe, secure, and loved.
Reading bedtime stories to children
is a great practice to build positive relationships
and cultivate peace and security.
Because I am aware that in this world,
too many children do not go to bed
feeling safe and secure,
I have decided that all proceeds
from the sale of this book
will go toward aiding the fight against human trafficking.
To learn more about the nonprofits
and organizations we are donating to, please visit
www.permacultureprincess.com/book

This book was inspired after I started to find scraps of paper throughout the house and in various file cabinets of little poems my dad had written. I dreamed of one day collecting his quirky quips and prose and putting them into a book. This dream was expanded when we found a friend who was willing to do illustrations. Our friend is not an illustrator, by trade, but he is a highly creative and adept learner of new skills. While his work is highly creditable, he has chosen to stay anonymous, and we honor his decision. I am forever grateful to those who have made this dream possible.

FOREWORD

He once worked in men's clothing at Gimbels on Main.
He once coached track and basketball games.

He spent time as a busboy, washing dishes in back.
His design for a candy bar made its way to store racks.

His catering company served food on a yacht.
He made fancy trays for parties a lot.

He drove heavy machinery for builders and more.
He played his hand at politics, won county supervisor.

He bought buildings and houses and started to invest.
He ran a restaurant in Milwaukee. When did he rest?

He oversaw planning for a modern wagon train.
He built a hobby farm on the Wisconsin plains.

Respected in his church, as an elder, he did sit.
He led Bible studies and taught from the pulpit.

But of all the jobs and roles that he's had,
his most important one was being a dad.

And if one day a little girl can picture,
sitting on Dad's knee, reading this literature,

then I will be reminded that God answers prayers.
For the love of a father inspired me to share.

After my first wish,
I caught my first fish.

I put it on a dish
and ate.

As I looked at the dish,

did I eat my first fish?

Or was it my first wish

I ate?

Katie did whatever she pleased. She climbed to the top of a chestnut tree.

She picked a bunch of humming leaves. Katydids, I do believe.

The 'I Don't Know' Animal

I looked.   It jumped.
No more could I see.
What I thought it was,
I hoped it not be.
A rat?
My size?
Could this be true?
My guide answered, trembling, "Kangaroo."

A picture I drew,
documenting it's name,
never giving
more thought
to this strange
looking game.

"Kangaroo," he called them.
I know that's what he said.
It was noted in my book
as I went off to bed.

Much later, I learned
how his answer rang true.
"I don't know"
is what he shouted
when he said
"Kangaroo."

"Kangaroo"

Randy Roach, so quick with speed,
thought he could lose no race.
Scurrying up the living room wall,
bragging none could keep his pace.
He asked of all, near and far,
for a competition to be.
But none in this world of creatures so small
could compete with a roach such as he.

Randy Roach

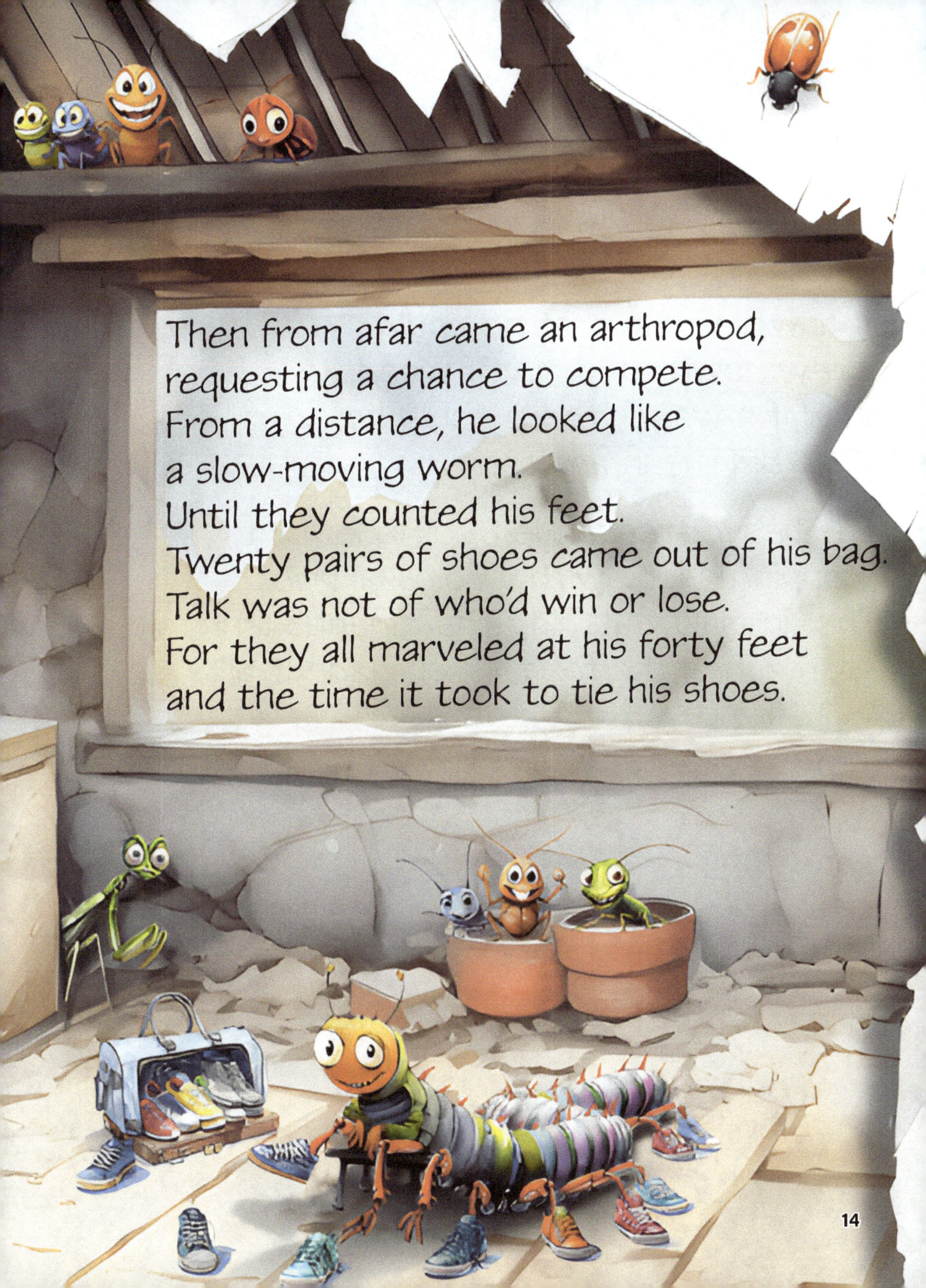

Then from afar came an arthropod,
requesting a chance to compete.
From a distance, he looked like
a slow-moving worm.
Until they counted his feet.
Twenty pairs of shoes came out of his bag.
Talk was not of who'd win or lose.
For they all marveled at his forty feet
and the time it took to tie his shoes.

SEQUOIA

A fox, being very sly,
asked the beaver as he happened by
if it were true that he could
chew down any tree of wood.
And if a wager there could be,
if he did mean any tree.

The beaver responded, to his delight,
dropping a limb with a colossal bite.
The animals watching the gigantic limb fall
approached the fox to mortgage it all.

They laughed at the fox on the way to the sight, imagining the winnings they'd have by night. Yet silence hit fast. This would not be the night they met the mighty sequoia tree.

A spider, hanging from his web,
wriggled his legs above my head.
I grabbed a book to squash him dead!
Decided to read
the book instead.

That's a Croc!

The little frog
jumped on a log,
never looking under.

Having fun,
out in the sun,
started to croak thunder.

The log, as you see,
was not from a tree
and only wanted to plunder.

As it opened its eyes, to the frog's surprise...

Snap!

The log slipped into slumber.

My Horse, Plastic

I named her because of her smooth brown coat.
What I am about to tell you is true.
Any stunt that you can conceive,
my dear brown horse can do.
My brown horse can float through the air,
with a little help from me.
I love her for her grace and flair.
She's been known to clear a tree.
She has done a rolling jump,
a flip in mid-air. All this is true.
There is not a stunt imagined
that Plastic cannot do.

Bird with a Flat Beak

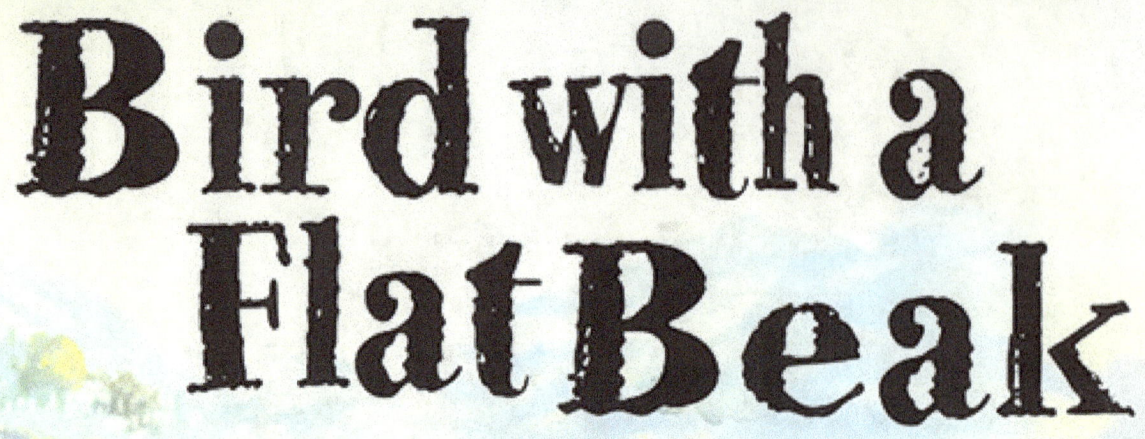

A bird with a bill
went for a swim.
A bird with a bill
observed it getting dim.

A bird with a bill looked to the sky,
discovered something falling
and heard someone cry...

"Duck!"

Doctor, doctor! Doctor Bill tried to get sick Phil a pill. Before he could, poor Phil fell ill. No more Phil for Bill to bill.

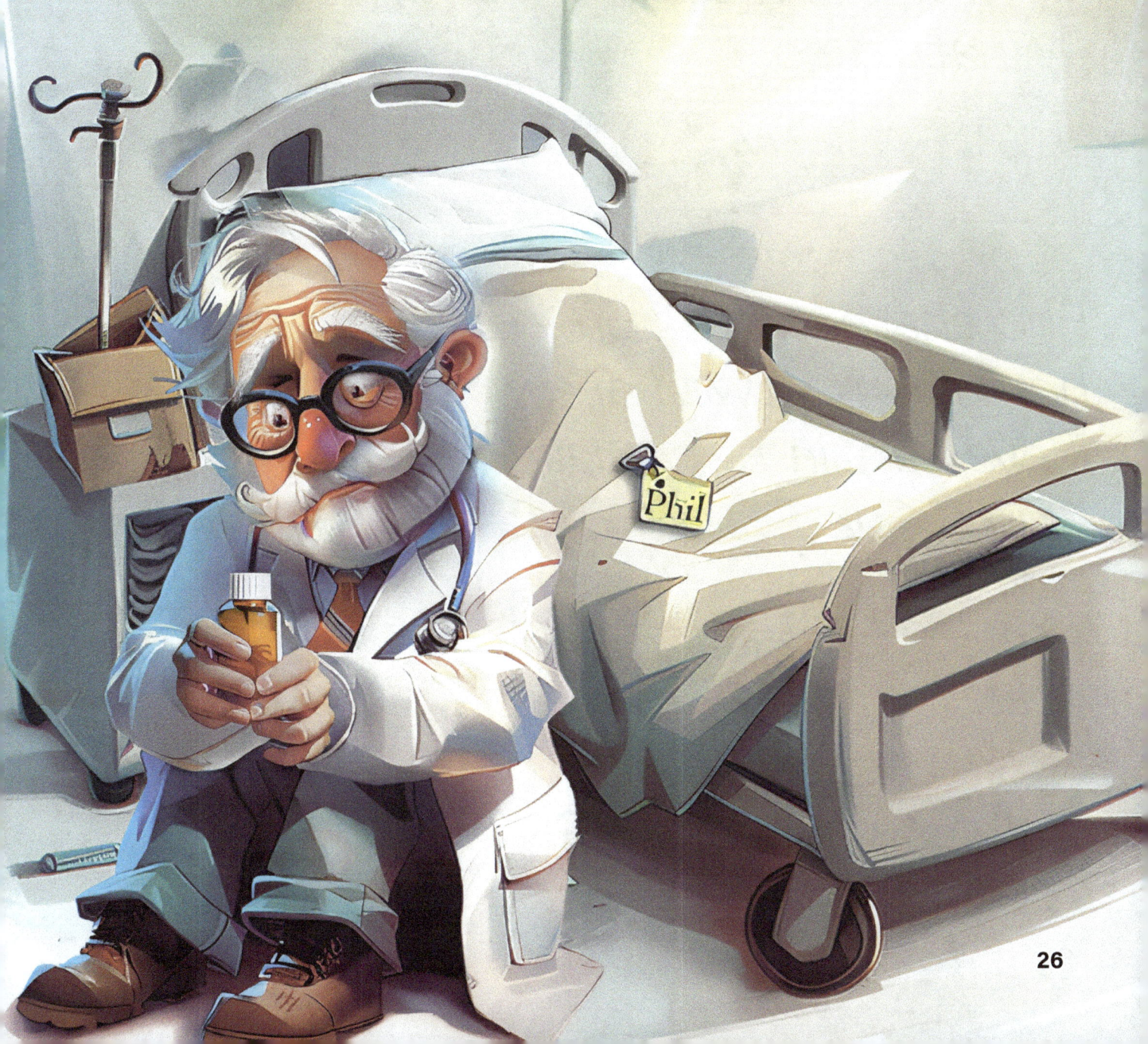

Stingy Sue

Stingy, stingy, stingy Sue
brewed some stew but never for two.
Had a friend over.
What to do?

She shared with Lou
her fresh-brewed stew.
Never again to be called
stingy Sue.

WILLOW'S

I asked if Willy would make a flute of willow wood. Willy said he could and would.

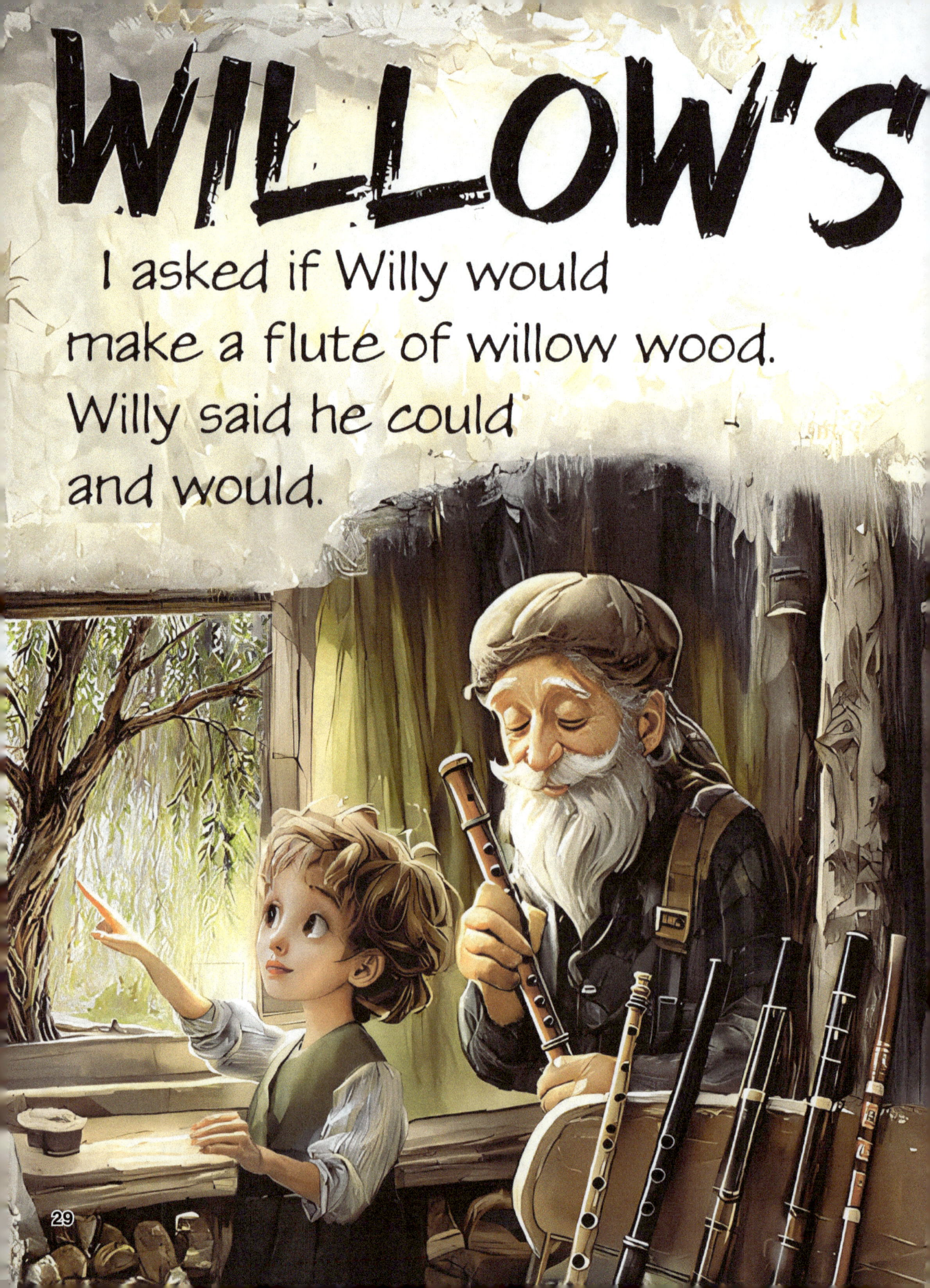

FLUTE

Only if I understood that willow wood could wilt and would.

TICKLISH TOES

Daddy's going to keep you warm.
He will hug you tight in his strong arms.

And when you're cozy
and about to sleep,
Daddy will tickle
both your feet.

PLATYPUS

A paleontologist,
I thought I would be.
So I started to unearth
every bone I did see.

I traveled down south
to peak under the ice,
came across an animal
that made me look twice.

I could not believe
what my eyes did see.
My attention so captured,
I ran into a tree.

A duck bill, a beaver tail,
claws like a bear?
It was a rare thing.
I saw it. I swear!

Could anything like this
monstrosity be true?
It slithered into the water,
like an otter would do.

It looked like every creature
rolled into one.
Surely, the platypus
was the Creator having fun.

An ant crawled
in my sugar bowl.
What was I to say?
For a time, I thought.
Then decided not.
He wouldn't listen anyway.

The Web

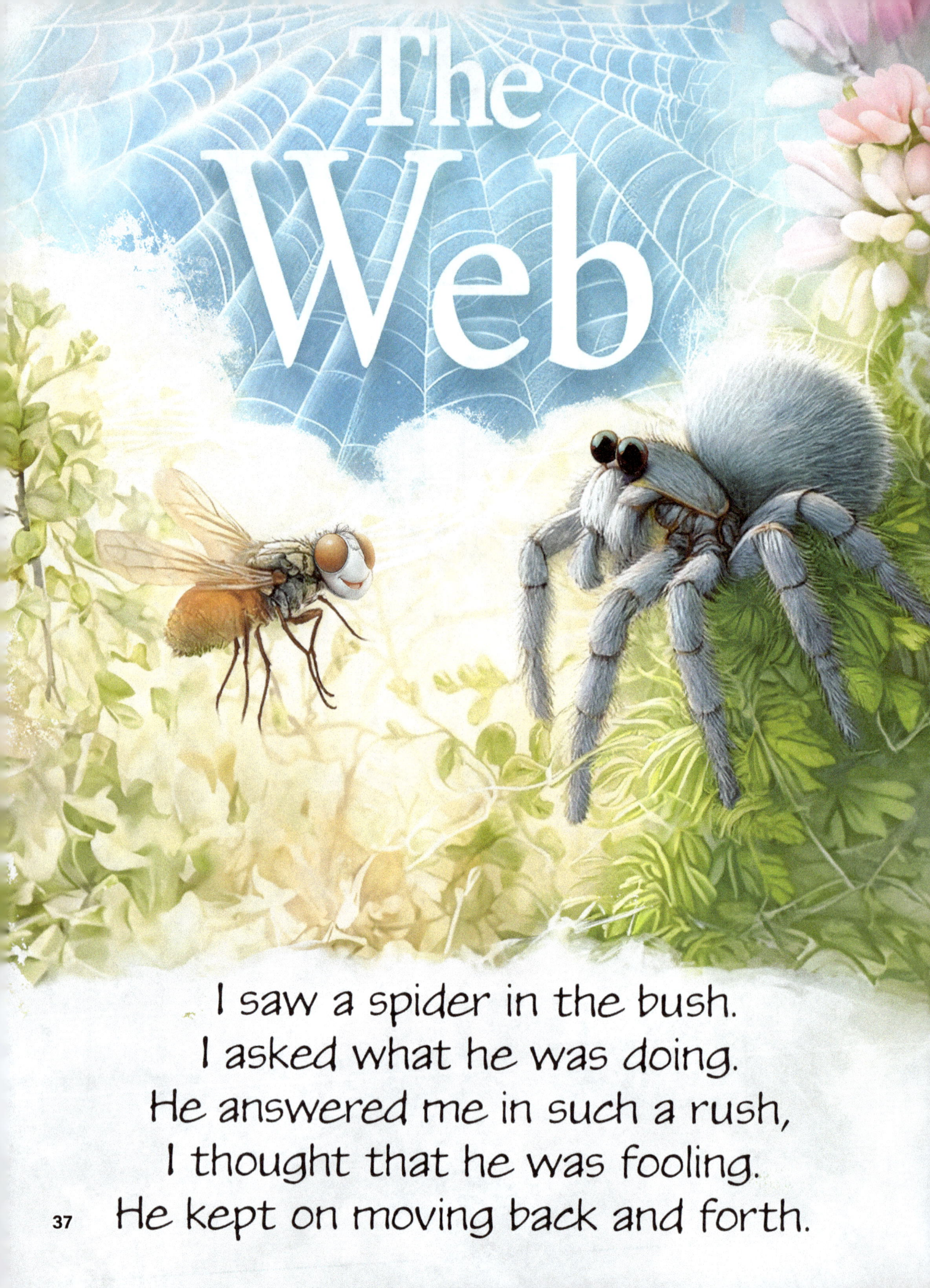

I saw a spider in the bush.
I asked what he was doing.
He answered me in such a rush,
I thought that he was fooling.
He kept on moving back and forth.

He said he was making a web.
I asked him why he made it so.
And this is what he said.
"Did you ever lie in a hammock?
It is the most comfortable of beds.
And if you'd like to try it now,
feel free. Go right ahead."

I thought about it for a while,
then remembered what my mother said.
"Watch out for the crafty spider,
especially his inviting web bed."

We're all Nuts

Squirrel up in the hickory tree.
Did you want to talk with me?

Or are you just keeping a watchful eye on every nut as they walk by?

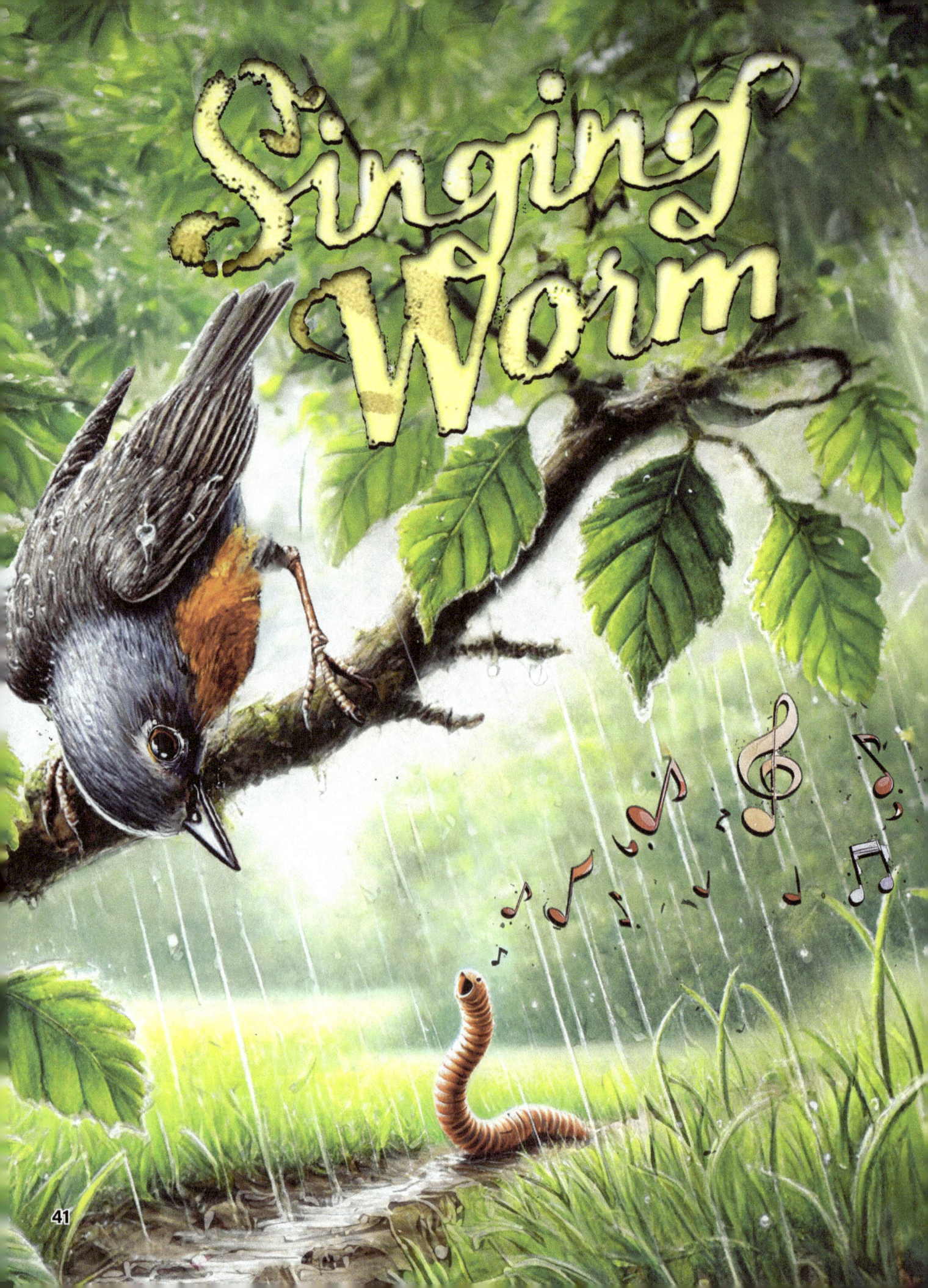

A worm whose thing it was to sing
sang beautiful songs of anything.
He sang too loud one rainy day,
awakening a bird, a robin, I'd say.
As the worm inched along,
never again to sing a song.

Tailor, tailor, tailor Bill
made a suit for his friend, Will.
Spun it out of golden yarn,
made him look like a charm.
A giant saw this golden charm.
Attached it to his clock alarm.
When it rang, it sent a chill
up the spine of poor Will,
whose friend
was Bill.

The Protein Filled Apple

I picked a red apple off of a tree,
bit into it. Tasty!
As tasty could be!
Chewed up that bite,
one big gulp.
It was gone.
My throat had a tickle.
Something felt wrong.
Looked at the apple.
Couldn't believe what was left!
Half of a wiggly worm,
portions more in a nest.

I was about to toss the apple away but remembered how tasty. What else can I say?

Apple Pie

Apple, apple,
apple pie.
Ate so much,
I thought I'd die.

SUE

Silly Sally's sister, Sue, wanted Barry to say "I do." She walked him to a church in town, only to find it had burned down.

She then went to the nearest judge but found that he was holding a grudge. The judge, after all, wanted Sue to be a wife for his little brother, Terry.

Meow

A little gray mouse jumped from rock to rock.
The pussycat was heard to say,

"Meow, meow. Meow, meow."

What Do You Like?

Pogo sticks.
Ice cream licks.
Apples and honey.
Basketballs. Climbing walls.
A piggy bank with money.
Jumping logs. Playing with dogs.
Swimming when it's sunny.
Watermelon treats.
Hotdogs and beets.

Wait!

Did I say beets?
That's not funny!
I meant
candy treats!
Does that mean
I'm growing up,
Mommy?

Sharing

I wished for a gift
that Santa could bring
to a little girl like me.
I made it clear.
I told him well
when I sat
upon his knee.

I asked for a doll, just for me,
with all the accessories.
Instead, I got a game to share
with my whole family.

I wondered hard.
I questioned why
Santa didn't listen to me
I did not get what I wanted most
or anything I thought should be.

I got what I needed to learn to share.
At least, that's what Mother told me.
I now know this: the most precious gift was not under the tree.
But when I shared my game with all, Santa must have heard me.

Orange Breasted Robin

    The night was cold and dreary,
lit only by starlight.
    Every knock brought the answer:
"Sorry, not a room tonight."
    The damp air called to all,
A warm fire there should be.
    A scream broke the night's silence
The two now became three.
    With the many needs and doings
that poor Joseph now did face.
    To make and fan the fire
was moved to second place.

    As Joseph prayed for guidance,
a little brown bird he did see.
    It proceeded to make a pile of twigs
from the many nearby trees.
    Joseph started a fire
but found it hard to keep aglow.
    Each time he tended to Mary's needs,
the flames of the fire grew low.

The little bird, now exhausted,
  after making the pile of wood,
flapped his wings to fan the flame,
  knowing the warmth would
    make them all feel good.
As the flames grew bright,
an orange glow appeared
on the little bird's breast.
As baby Jesus awoke to the warmth,
  the tiny bird, He did bless.
From now and forever, for the world to see,
  for all generations to know,
there's an orange crest on the little bird's breast.
  And the warmth of spring will follow.

My Greater Sin

A little boy went into the store.
Stole some soup, ran out the door.
Officer Tim chased him down,
And brought him back, with a frown.

Mr. O'Neal asked "Why'd you steal?"
The boy replied, "My mother's ill."
The crowd began, "Send him to jail!
He's just a liar, and bound to fail."

As Officer Tim reached for cuffs,
Mr. O'Neal shouted, "That's enough!"
He gave the boy more soup and medicine,
Gently whispered, "Stealing is a sin,
But not as great as mine,
If we don't make sure
that your mother is fine."

FROM THE ILLUSTRATOR

It is with great honor to have this dedicated page
to share a humble thought with all of you.
The challenge of illustrating each perfect poem
soon led me to writing my own.
If you happen to feel that same inspiration too,
we've left the next couple of pages just for you.
Be Inspired and Write a Poem!

www.ingramcontent.com/pod-product-compliance
Lightning Source LLC
Chambersburg PA
CBHW060410010526
44107CB00005B/640